*Paracelsus,
the Four Elements
and Their Spirits*

By
Manly P. Hall

Copyright © 2021 Lamp of Trismegistus. All rights reserved. No part of this publication may be reproduced or transmitted in any form or by any means, electronic or mechanical, including photocopying, recording, or by any information storage and retrieval system, without permission in writing from Lamp of Trismegistus. Reviewers may quote brief passages.

ISBN: 978-1-63118-400-0

Esoteric Classics

Other Books in this Series and Related Titles

Aurora of the Philosophers by Paracelsus (978-1-63118-507-6)

Rosicrucian Rules, Secret Signs, Codes and Symbols by various (978-1-63118-488-8)

On the Philadelphian Gold by Philochrysus & Philadelphus (978-1-63118-511-3)

The Secret Book of the Philosopher's Stone by Artephius (978-1-63118-517-5)

The Stone of the Philosophers by A E Waite (978-1-63118-509-0)

Freher's Process in the Philosophical Work by D A Freher (978-1-63118-484-0)

The Comte de St. Germain: The Secret of Kings (978-1-63118-525-0)

The Rosicrucian Chemical Marriage by Christian Rosenkreuz (978-1-63118-458-1)

The Alchemical Catechism of Paracelsus by Paracelsus (978-1-63118-513-7)

Alchemy in the Nineteenth Century by Helena P. Blavatsky (978-1-63118-446-8)

Rosicrucians and Speculative Masonry in the Seventeenth Century (978-1-63118-489-5)

Qabbalistic Teachings and the Tree of Life by M P Hall (978-1-63118-482-6)

The Sepher Yetzirah and the Qabalah by M P Hall (978-1-63118-481-9)

The Devil in Love by Jacques Cazotte (978–1–63118–499–4)

History, Analysis and Secret Tradition of the Tarot by Hall &c (978-1-63118-445-1)

Crystal Vision Through Crystal Gazing by Frater Achad (978-1-63118-455-0)

The Golden Verses of Pythagoras: Five Translations (978-1-63118-479-6)

Arcane Formulas or Mental Alchemy by W W Atkinson (978-1-63118-459-8)

Hermetic Arcanum by Jean d'Espagnet (978-1-63118-519-9)

The A E Waite Reader: A Selection of Occult Essays (978-1-63118-515-1)

The Leadbeater Reader: A Selection of Occult Essays (978-1-63118-483-3)

Audio versions are also available on Audible, Amazon and Apple

Other Books in this Series and Related Titles

On the Cave of the Nymphs in the Odyssey by Thomas Taylor (978-1-63118-505-2)

The Poem of Hashish by A Crowley & C Baudelaire (978-1-63118-484-0)

Brothers & Builders by Joseph Fort Newton (978-1-63118-506-9)

The Kabbalah of Masonry & Related Writings by E Levi &c (978-1-63118-453-6)

A Collection of Fiction and Essays by Occult Writers on Supernatural and Metaphysical Subjects by various (978–1–63118–510–6)

Clairvoyance and Psychic Abilities by A Besant &c (978-1-63118-403-1)

Cloud Upon the Sanctuary by Waite & K Eckartshausen (978-1-63118-438-3)

The Hymns of Hermes by G. R. S. Mead (978-1-63118-405-5)

The Secrets of Enoch by Enoch (978-1-63118-449-9)

Masonic and Rosicrucian History by M P Hall & H Voorhis (978-1-63118-486-4)

The Sword of Welleran and Other Stories by Lord Dunsany (978-1-63118-501-4)

The Janeites, The Man Who Would Be King and Other Stories of Freemasonry by Rudyard Kipling (978–1–63118–480–2)

Gnosis of the Mind by G. R. S. Mead (978-1-63118-408-6)

The First and Second Gospels of the Infancy of Jesus Christ by Thomas and James (978-1-63118-415-4)

The Life of Pythagoras by Porphyry (978-1-63118-512-0)

Freemasonry & Catholicism by Max Heindel (978-1-63118-508-3)

The Feminine Occult by various authors (978-1-63118-711-7)

The Influence of Pythagoras on Freemasonry and Other Essays (978-1-63118-404-8)

The Path of Light: A Manual of Maha-Yana Buddhism (978-1-63118-471-0)

Tao Te Ching & Commentary by Lao Tzu & C Johnston (978-1-63118-495-6)

Audio versions are also available on Audible, Amazon and Apple

Table of Contents

Introduction...7

Paracelsus, the Four Elements and Their Spirits

Part I: Prologue...11

Part II: The Gnomes...19

Part III: The Undines...25

Part IV: The Salamanders...29

Part V: The Sylphs...33

Part VI: General Observations...37

INTRODUCTION

The word "esoteric" can be difficult to define. Esotericism in general can be seen less as a system of beliefs and more as a category, which encompasses numerous, different systems of beliefs. It's a bit of juxtaposition, since the word "esoteric" indicates something that few people know about, while the term itself broadly covers numerous philosophies, practices, areas of study and belief systems.

In a greater sense, Esotericism acts as a storehouse for secret knowledge, which is often considered ancient *(by tradition, if not by fact),* passed down from generation to generation, in private. At various times in history, simply possessing the knowledge of some of these subjects, was considered illegal and a jailable offence, if discovered. This usually included such general topics as Alchemy, Pharmacology, Qabalah, Hermeticism, Occultism, Ceremonial Magic, Astrology, Divination, Rosicrucianism and so on. Collectively, these areas of study were often referred to as the esoteric sciences.

Sometimes, the outer garment of a subject isn't esoteric, while what is hidden beneath it, is. As an example, Freemasonry isn't necessarily esoteric by nature (at *least not anymore),* but certain signs, passwords and handshakes given to the candidate during their initiation, are in fact, esoteric, in the sense that they are hidden from the general public.

Today, in the twenty-first century, such topics are readily available at bookstores across the country, and numerous mainsteam publishers offer beginners guides and coffee-table volumes on many of these subjects, intended for mass appeal. Books like *"The Secret"* have turned previously arcane topics into household knowledge. All that being the case, however, it isn't to say that there still aren't buried secrets to uncover, ancient wisdom being ignored and forgotten mysteries to be explored. In fact, it is often that we are only able to further our own studies by standing on the shoulders of these disappearing giants.

Lamp of Trismegistus is doing its part to help preserve humanity's esoteric history by making some of these classics available to those students who are seeking to unearth the knowledge of these ancient colossi.

So, be sure to check other titles from our *Esoteric Classics* series, as well as our *Occult Fiction, Theosophical Classics, Foundations of Freemasonry Series, Supernatural Fiction, Paranormal Research Series, Studies in Buddhism* and our *Christian Apocrypha Series*. You can also download the audio versions of most of these titles from Amazon, Apple or Audible, for learning on the go.

PARACELSUS[1]

---

[1] **Born** Philippus Aureolus Theophrastus Bombastus von Hohenheim

PARACELSUS, THE FOUR ELEMENTS AND THEIR SPIRITS

PART I:
PROLOGUE

For the most comprehensive and lucid exposition of occult pneumatology[2] extant, mankind is indebted to Philippus Aureolus Paracelsus, prince of alchemists and Hermetic philosophers and true possessor of the *Royal Secret*.[3] Paracelsus believed that each of the four primary elements known to the ancients[4] consisted of a subtle, vaporous principle and a gross corporeal substance.

Air is, therefore, twofold in nature-tangible atmosphere and an intangible, volatile substratum which may be termed *spiritual air*. Fire is visible and invisible, discernible and indiscernible--a spiritual, ethereal flame manifesting through a material, substantial flame. Carrying the analogy further, water consists of a dense fluid and a potential essence of a fluidic nature. Earth has likewise two essential parts-- the lower being fixed, terreous, immobile; the higher, rarefied, mobile, and virtual. The general term "elements" has been applied to the lower, or physical, phases of these four primary principles, and the name elemental essences to their corresponding invisible, spiritual constitutions. Minerals, plants, animals, and men live

---

[2] the branch of philosophy dealing with spiritual substances
[3] the Philosopher's Stone and the Elixir of Life
[4] earth, fire, air, and water

in a world composed of the gross side of these four elements, and from various combinations of them construct their living organisms.

Henry Drummond, in *Natural Law in the Spiritual World*, describes this process as follows: "If we analyze this material point at which all life starts, we shall find it to consist of a clear structure-less, jelly-like substance resembling albumen or white of egg. It is made of Carbon, Hydrogen, Oxygen and Nitrogen. Its name is protoplasm. And it is not only the structural unit with which all living bodies start in life, but with which they are subsequently built up. 'Protoplasm,' says Huxley, 'simple or nucleated, is the formal basis of all life. It is the clay of the Potter.'"

The *water* element of the ancient philosophers has been metamorphosed into the hydrogen of modern science; the *air* has become oxygen; the *fire*, nitrogen; the *earth*, carbon.

Just as visible Nature is populated by an infinite number of living creatures, so, according to Paracelsus, the invisible, spiritual counterpart of visible Nature[5] is inhabited by a host of peculiar beings, to whom he has given the name elementals, and which have later been termed the Nature spirits. Paracelsus divided these people of the elements into four distinct groups, which he called *gnomes, undines, sylphs,* and *salamanders*. He taught that they were really living entities, many resembling human beings in shape, and inhabiting worlds of their own, unknown to man because his undeveloped senses were incapable of functioning beyond the limitations of the grosser elements.

---

[5] composed of the tenuous principles of the visible elements

The civilizations of Greece, Rome, Egypt, China, and India believed implicitly in satyrs, sprites, and goblins. They peopled the sea with mermaids, the rivers and fountains with nymphs, the air with fairies, the fire with Lares and Penates, and the earth with fauns, dryads, and hamadryads. These Nature spirits were held in the highest esteem, and propitiatory offerings were made to them. Occasionally, as the result of atmospheric conditions or the peculiar sensitiveness of the devotee, they became visible. Many authors wrote concerning them in terms which signify that they had actually beheld these inhabitants of Nature's finer realms. A number of authorities are of the opinion that many of the gods worshiped by the pagans were elementals, for some of these *invisibles* were believed to be of commanding stature and magnificent deportment.

The Greeks gave the name *dæmon* to some of these elementals, especially those of the higher orders, and worshiped them. Probably the most famous of these *dæmons* is the mysterious spirit which instructed Socrates, and of whom that great philosopher spoke in the highest terms. Those who have devoted much study to the invisible constitution of man realize that it is quite probable the dæmon of Socrates and the angel of Jacob Boehme were in reality not elementals, but the overshadowing divine natures of these philosophers themselves. In his notes to *Apuleius on the God of Socrates,* Thomas Taylor says:

> "As the dæmon of Socrates, therefore, was doubtless one of the highest order, as may be inferred from the intellectual superiority of Socrates to most other men,

Apuleius is justified in calling this dæmon a God. And that the dæmon of Socrates indeed was divine, is evident from the testimony of Socrates himself in the First Alcibiades: for in the course of that dialogue he clearly says, 'I have long been of the opinion that the God did not as yet direct me to hold any conversation with you.' And in the Apology he most unequivocally evinces that this dæmon is allotted a divine transcendency, considered as ranking in the order of dæmons."

The idea once held, that the invisible elements surrounding and interpenetrating the earth were peopled with living, intelligent beings, may seem ridiculous to the prosaic mind of today. This doctrine, however, has found favor with some of the greatest intellects of the world. The sylphs of Facius Cardan, the philosopher of Milan; the salamander seen by Benvenuto Cellini; the pan of St. Anthony; and *le petit homme rouge*[6] of Napoleon Bonaparte, have found their places in the pages of history.

Literature has also perpetuated the concept of Nature spirits. The mischievous Puck of Shakespeare's *Midsummer Night's Dream;* the elementals of Alexander Pope's Rosicrucian poem, *The Rape of the Lock,* the mysterious creatures of Lord Lytton's *Zanoni;* James Barrie's immortal Tinker Bell; and the famous bowlers that Rip Van Winkle encountered in the Catskill Mountains, are well-known characters to students of literature. The folklore and mythology of all peoples abound in legends concerning these mysterious little figures who haunt

---

[6] the little red man, or gnome

old castles, guard treasures in the depths of the earth, and build their homes under the spreading protection of toadstools. Fairies are the delight of childhood, and most children give them up with reluctance. Not so very long ago the greatest minds of the world believed in the existence of fairies, and it is still an open question as to whether Plato, Socrates, and Iamblichus were wrong when they avowed their reality.

Paracelsus, when describing the substances which constitute the bodies of the elementals, divided flesh into two kinds, the first being that which we have all inherited through Adam. This is the visible, corporeal flesh. The second was that flesh which had not descended from Adam and, being more attenuated, was not subject to the limitations of the former. The bodies of the elementals were composed of this transubstantial flesh. Paracelsus stated that there is as much difference between the bodies of men and the bodies of the Nature spirits as there is between matter and spirit.

"Yet," he adds, "the Elementals are not spirits, because they have flesh, blood and bones; they live and propagate offspring; they eat and talk, act and sleep, &c., and consequently they cannot be properly called 'spirits.' They are beings occupying a place between men and spirits, resembling men and spirits, resembling men and women in their organization and form, and resembling spirits in the rapidity of their locomotion." Later the same author calls these creatures *composita,* inasmuch as the substance out of which they are composed seems to be a composite of spirit and matter. He uses color to explain the idea. Thus, the mixture of blue and red gives purple, a new color, resembling neither of the others yet composed of both. Such is the case with the Nature spirits; they resemble neither spiritual creatures nor material beings, yet are composed of the substance which we may call *spiritual matter*, or ether.

Paracelsus further adds that whereas man is composed of several natures[7] combined in one unit, the elemental has but one *principle,* the ether out of which it is composed and in which it lives. The reader must remember that by *ether* is meant the spiritual essence of one of the four elements. There are as many ethers as there are elements and as many distinct families of Nature spirits as there are ethers. These families are completely isolated in their own ether and have no intercourse with the denizens of the other ethers; but, as man has within his own nature centers of consciousness sensitive to the impulses of all the four ethers, it is possible for any of the elemental kingdoms to communicate with him under proper conditions.

The Nature spirits cannot be destroyed by the grosser elements, such as material fire, earth, air, or water, for they function in a rate of vibration higher than that of earthy substances. Being composed of only one element or principle,[8] they have no immortal spirit and at death merely disintegrate back into the element from which they were originally individualized. No individual consciousness is preserved after death, for there is no superior vehicle present to contain it. Being made of but one substance, there is no friction between vehicles: thus there is little wear or tear incurred by their bodily functions, and they therefore live to great age. Those composed

---

[7] spirit, soul, mind, and body
[8] the ether in which they function

of earth ether are the shortest lived; those composed of air ether, the longest. The average length of life is between three hundred and a thousand years. Paracelsus maintained that they live in conditions similar to our earth environments, and are somewhat subject to disease. These creatures are thought to be incapable of spiritual development, but most of them are of a high moral character.

Concerning the elemental ethers in which the Nature spirits exist, Paracelsus wrote: "They live in the four elements: the Nymphs in the element of water, the Sylphs in that of the air, the Pigmies in the earth, and the Salamanders in fire. They are also called Undines, Sylvestres, Gnomes, Vulcani, etc. Each species moves only in the element to which it belongs, and neither of them can go out of its appropriate element, which is to them as the air is to us, or the water to fishes; and none of them can live in the element belonging to another class. To each elemental being the element in which it lives is transparent, invisible and respirable, as the atmosphere is to ourselves."

The reader should be careful not to confuse the Nature spirits with the true life waves evolving through the invisible worlds. While the elementals are composed of only one etheric (or atomic) essence, the angels, archangels, and other superior, transcendental entities have composite organisms, consisting of a spiritual nature and a chain of vehicles to express that nature not unlike those of men, but not including the physical body with its attendant limitations.

To the philosophy of Nature spirits is generally attributed an Eastern origin, probably Brahmanic; and Paracelsus secured his knowledge of them from Oriental sages with whom he came in contact during his lifetime of philosophical wanderings. The Egyptians and Greeks gleaned their information from the same source. The four main divisions of Nature spirits must now be considered separately, according to the teachings of Paracelsus and the Abbé de Villars[9] and such scanty writings of other authors as are available.

---

[9] See *Comte de Gabalis*

PART II:
THE GNOMES

The elementals who dwell in that attenuated body of the earth which is called the terreous ether are grouped together under the general heading of *gnomes*.[10]

Just as there are many types of human beings evolving through the objective physical elements of Nature, so there are many types of gnomes evolving through the subjective ethereal body of Nature. These earth spirits work in an element so close in vibratory rate to the material earth that they have immense power over its rocks and flora, and also over the mineral elements in the animal and human kingdoms. Some, like the pygmies, work with the stones, gems, and metals, and are supposed to be the guardians of hidden treasures. They live in caves, far down in what the Scandinavians called the Land of the Nibelungen. In Wagner's wonderful opera cycle, *The Ring of the Nibelungen*, Alberich makes himself King of the Pygmies and forces these little creatures to gather for him the treasures concealed beneath the surface of the earth.

Besides the pygmies there are other gnomes, who are called tree and forest sprites. To this group belong the sylvestres, satyrs, pans, dryads, hamadryads, durdalis, elves, brownies, and little old men of the woods. Paracelsus states that the gnomes build houses of substances resembling in their constituencies alabaster, marble, and cement, but the true

---

[10] The name is probably derived from the Greek *genomus*, meaning earth dweller.

nature of these materials is unknown, having no counterpart in physical nature. Some families of gnomes gather in communities, while others are indigenous to the substances with and in which they work. For example, the hamadryads live and die with the plants or trees of which they are a part. Every shrub and flower is said to have its own Nature spirit, which often uses the physical body of the plant as its habitation. The ancient philosophers, recognizing the principle of intelligence manifesting itself in every department of Nature alike, believed that the quality of natural selection exhibited by creatures not possessing organized mentalities expressed in reality the decisions of the Nature spirits themselves.

C. M. Gayley, in *The Classic Myths,* says: "It was a pleasing trait in the old paganism that it loved to trace in every operation of nature the agency of deity. The imagination of the Greeks peopled the regions of earth and sea with divinities, to whose agency it attributed the phenomena that our philosophy ascribes to the operation of natural law." Thus, in behalf of the plant it worked with, the elemental accepted and rejected food elements, deposited coloring matter therein, preserved and protected the seed, and performed many other beneficent offices. Each species was served by a different but appropriate type of Nature spirit. Those working with poisonous shrubs, for example, were offensive in their appearance. It is said the Nature spirits of poison hemlock resemble closely tiny human skeletons, thinly covered with a semi-transparent flesh. They live in and through the hemlock, and if it be cut down remain with the broken shoots until both die, but while there is the slightest evidence of life in the shrub it shows the presence of the elemental guardian.

Great trees also have their Nature spirits, but these are much larger than the elementals of smaller plants. The labors of the pygmies include the cutting of the crystals in the rocks and the development of veins of ore. When the gnomes are laboring with animals or human beings, their work is confined to the tissues corresponding with their own natures. Hence they work with the bones, which belong to the mineral kingdom, and the ancients believed the reconstruction of broken members to be impossible without the cooperation of the elementals.

The gnomes are of various sizes--most of them much smaller than human beings, though some of them have the power of changing their stature at will. This is the result of the extreme mobility of the element in which they function. Concerning them the Abbé de Villars wrote: "The earth is filled well nigh to its center with Gnomes, people of slight stature, who are the guardians of treasures, minerals and precious stones. They are ingenious, friends of man, and easy to govern."

Not all authorities agree concerning the amiable disposition of the gnomes. Many state that they are of a tricky and malicious nature, difficult to manage, and treacherous. Writers agree, however, that when their confidence is won they are faithful and true. The philosophers and initiates of the ancient world were instructed concerning these mysterious little people and were taught how to communicate with them and gain their cooperation in undertakings of importance. The magi were always warned, however, never to betray the trust of the elementals, for if they did, the invisible creatures, working through the subjective nature of man, could cause them endless sorrow and probably ultimate destruction. So long as the mystic served others, the gnomes would serve him, but if he sought to use their aid selfishly to gain temporal power they would turn upon him with unrelenting fury. The same was true if he sought to deceive them.

The earth spirits meet at certain times of the year in great conclaves, as Shakespeare suggests in his Midsummer Night's Dream, where the elementals all gather to rejoice in the beauty and harmony of Nature and the prospects of an excellent harvest. The gnomes are ruled over by a king, whom they greatly love and revere. His name is *Gob;* hence his subjects are often called goblins. Mediæval mystics gave a corner of creation[11] to each of the four kingdoms of Nature spirits, and because of their earthy character the gnomes were assigned to the North--the place recognized by the ancients as the source of darkness and death. One of the four main divisions of human disposition was also assigned to the gnomes, and because so many of them dwelt in the darkness of caves and the gloom of forests their temperament was said to be melancholy, gloomy, and despondent. By this it is not meant that they themselves are of such disposition, but rather that they have special control over elements of similar consistency.

The gnomes marry and have families, and the female gnomes are called *gnomides*. Some wear clothing woven of the

---

[11] one of the cardinal points

element in which they live. In other instances their garments are part of themselves and grow with them, like the fur of animals. The gnomes are said to have insatiable appetites, and to spend a great part of the time eating, but they earn their food by diligent and conscientious labor. Most of them are of a miserly temperament, fond of storing things away in secret places. There is abundant evidence of the fact that small children often see the gnomes, inasmuch as their contact with the material side of Nature is not yet complete and they still function more or less consciously in the invisible worlds.

CONVENTIONAL GNOMES.[12]

---

[12] From Gjellerup's *Den Ældre Eddas Gudesange*. The type of gnome most frequently seen is the brownie, or elf, a mischievous and grotesque little creature from twelve to eighteen inches high, usually dressed in green or russet brown. Most of them appear as very aged, often with long white beards, and their figures are inclined to rotundity. They can be seen scampering out of holes in the stumps of trees and sometimes they vanish by actually dissolving into the tree itself.

According to Paracelsus, "Man lives in the exterior elements and the Elementals live in the interior elements. The latter have dwellings and clothing, manners and customs, languages and governments of their own, in the same sense as the bees have their queens and herds of animals their leaders."

Paracelsus differs somewhat from the Greek mystics concerning the environmental limitations imposed on the Nature spirits. The Swiss philosopher constitutes them of subtle invisible ethers. According to this hypothesis they would be visible only at certain times and only to those *en rapport* with their ethereal vibrations. The Greeks, on the other hand, apparently believed that many Nature spirits had material constitutions capable of functioning in the physical world. Often the recollection of a dream is so vivid that, upon awakening, a person actually believes that he has passed through a physical experience. The difficulty of accurately judging as to the end of physical sight and the beginning of ethereal vision may account for these differences of opinion.

Even this explanation, however, does not satisfactorily account for the satyr which, according to St. Jerome, was captured alive during the reign of Constantine and exhibited to the people. It was of human form with the horns and feet of a goat. After its death it was preserved in salt and taken to the Emperor that he might testify to its reality.[13]

---

[13] It is within the bounds of probability that this curiosity was what modern science knows as a *monstrosity*.

PART III:
THE UNDINES

As the gnomes were limited in their function to the elements of the earth, so the undines[14] function in the invisible, spiritual essence called humid[15] ether. In its vibratory rate this is close to the element water, and so the undines are able to control, to a great degree, the course and function of this fluid in Nature. Beauty seems to be the keynote of the water spirits. Wherever we find them pictured in art or sculpture, they abound in symmetry and grace. Controlling the water element--which has always been a feminine symbol--it is natural that the water spirits should most often be symbolized as female.

There are many groups of undines. Some inhabit waterfalls, where they can be seen in the spray; others are indigenous to swiftly moving rivers; some have their habitat in dripping, oozing fens or marshes; while other groups dwell in clear mountain lakes. According to the philosophers of antiquity, every fountain had its nymph; every ocean wave its oceanid. The water spirits were known under such names as oreades, nereides, limoniades, naiades, water sprites, sea maids, mermaids, and potamides. Often the water nymphs derived their names from the streams, lakes, or seas in which they dwelt.

In describing them, the ancients agreed on certain salient features. In general, nearly all the undines closely resembled human beings in appearance and size, though the ones

---

[14] a name given to the family of water elementals
[15] or liquid

inhabiting small streams and fountains were of correspondingly lesser proportions. It was believed that these water spirits were occasionally capable of assuming the appearance of normal human beings and actually associating with men and women. There are many legends about these spirits and their adoption by the families of fishermen, but in nearly every case the undines heard the call of the waters and returned to the realm of Neptune, the King of the Sea.

A MERMAID.[16]

Practically nothing is known concerning the male undines. The water spirits did not establish homes in the same

---

[16] From Lycosthenes' *Prodigiorum ac Ostentorum Chronicon*. Probably the most famous of the undines were the mythological mermaids, with which early mariners peopled the Seven Seas. Belief in the existence of these creatures, the upper half of their bodies human in form and the lower half fishlike, may have been inspired by flocks of penguins seen at great distance, or possibly seals. In mediæval descriptions of mermaids, it was also stated that their hair was green like seaweed and that they wore wreaths twisted from the blossoms of subaqueous plants and sea anemones.

way that the gnomes did, but lived in coral caves under the ocean or among the reeds growing on the banks of rivers or the shores of lakes. Among the Celts there is a legend to the effect that Ireland was peopled, before the coming of its present inhabitants, by a strange race of semi-divine creatures; with the coming of the modem Celts they retired into the marshes and fens, where they remain even to this day. Diminutive undines lived under lily pads and in little houses of moss sprayed by waterfalls. The undines worked with the vital essences and liquids in plants, animals, and human beings, and were present in everything containing water. When seen, the undines generally resembled the goddesses of Greek statuary. They rose from the water draped in mist and could not exist very long apart from it.

There are many families of undines, each with its peculiar limitations, it is impossible to consider them here in detail. Their ruler, *Necksa,* they love and honor, and serve untiringly. Their temperament is said to be vital, and to them has been given as their throne the western corner of creation. They are rather emotional beings, friendly to human life and fond of serving mankind. They are sometimes pictured riding on dolphins or other great fish and seem to have a special love of flowers and plants, which they serve almost as devotedly and intelligently as the gnomes. Ancient poets have said that the songs of the undines were heard in the West Wind and that their lives were consecrated to the beautifying of the material earth.

PART IV:
THE SALAMANDERS

The third group of elementals is the salamanders, or spirits of fire, who live in that attenuated, spiritual ether which is the invisible fire element of Nature. Without them material fire cannot exist; a match cannot be struck nor will flint and steel give off their spark without the assistance of a salamander, who immediately appears,[17] evoked by friction. Man is unable to communicate successfully with the salamanders, owing to the fiery element in which they dwell, for everything is resolved to ashes that comes into their presence. By specially prepared compounds of herbs and perfumes the philosophers of the ancient world manufactured many kinds of incense. When incense was burned, the vapors which arose were especially suitable as a medium for the expression of these elementals, who, by borrowing the ethereal effluvium from the incense smoke, were able to make their presence felt.

The salamanders are as varied in their grouping and arrangement as either the undines or the gnomes. There are many families of them, differing in appearance, size, and dignity. Sometimes the salamanders were visible as small balls of light. Paracelsus says: "Salamanders have been seen in the shapes of fiery balls, or tongues of fire, running over the fields or peering in houses."

Mediæval investigators of the Nature spirits were of the opinion that the most common form of salamander was lizard-

---

[17] so the mediæval mystics believed

like in shape, a foot or more in length, and visible as a glowing Urodela, twisting and crawling in the midst of the fire. Another

A SALAMANDER, ACCORDING TO PARACELSUS.[18]

group was described as huge flaming giants in flowing robes, protected with sheets of fiery armor. Certain mediæval

---

[18] From Paracelsus' *Auslegung von 30 magischen Figuren.* The Egyptians, Chaldeans, and Persians often mistook the salamanders for gods, because of their radiant splendor and great power. The Greeks, following the example of earlier nations, deified the fire spirits and in their honor kept incense and altar fire, burning perpetually.

authorities, among them the Abbé de Villars,[19] held that Zarathustra[20] was the son of Vesta[21] and the great salamander Oromasis. Hence, from that time onward, undying fires have been maintained upon the Persian altars in honor of Zarathustra's flaming father.

One most important subdivision of the salamanders was the Acthnici. These creatures appeared only as indistinct globes. They were supposed to float over water at night and occasionally to appear as forks of flame on the masts and rigging of ships.[22] The salamanders were the strongest and most powerful of the elementals, and had as their ruler a magnificent flaming spirit called *Djin,*[23] terrible and awe-inspiring in appearance. The salamanders were dangerous and the sages were warned to keep away from them, as the benefits derived from studying them were often not commensurate with the price paid. As the ancients associated heat with the South, this corner of creation was assigned to the salamanders as their drone, and they exerted special influence over all beings of fiery or tempestuous temperament. In both animals and men, the salamanders work through the emotional nature by means of the body heat, the liver, and the blood stream. Without their assistance there would be no warmth.

---

[19] See *Comte de Gabalis*
[20] Zoroaster
[21] believed to have been the wife of Noah
[22] St. Elmo's fire
[23] Jinn romanized as djinn or anglicized as genie (*with the broader meaning of spirit or demon, depending on source*) are supernatural creatures in early pre-Islamic Arabian and later Islamic mythology and theology.

PART V:
THE SYLPHS

While the sages said that the fourth class of elementals, or sylphs, lived in the element of air, they meant by this not the natural atmosphere of the earth, but the invisible, intangible, spiritual medium--an ethereal substance similar in composition to our atmosphere, but far more subtle. In the last discourse of Socrates, as preserved by Plato in his *Phædo,* the condemned philosopher says:

"And upon the earth are animals and men, some in a middle region, others[24] dwelling about the air as we dwell about the sea; others in islands which the air flows round, near the continent; and in a word, the air is used by them as the water and the sea are by us, and the ether is to them what the air is to us. Moreover, the temperament of their seasons is such that they have no disease,[25] and live much longer than we do, and have sight and hearing and smell, and all the other senses, in far greater perfection, in the same degree that air is purer than water or the ether than air. Also they have temples and sacred places in which the gods really dwell, and they hear their voices and receive their answers, and are conscious of them and hold converse with them, and they see the sun, moon, and stars as they really are, and their other blessedness is of a piece with this." While the sylphs were believed to live among the clouds

---

[24] elementals
[25] Paracelsus disputes this

and in the surrounding air, their true home was upon the tops of mountains.

In his editorial notes to the *Occult Sciences* of Salverte, Anthony Todd Thomson says: "The Fayes and Fairies are evidently of Scandinavian origin, although the name of Fairy is supposed to be derived from, or rather is a modification of the Persian Peri, an imaginary benevolent being, whose province it was to guard men from the maledictions of evil spirits; but with more probability it may be referred to the Gothic Fagur, as the term Elves is from Alfa, the general appellation for the whole tribe. If this derivation of the name of Fairy be admitted, we may date the commencement of the popular belief in British Fairies to the period of the Danish conquest. They were supposed to be diminutive aerial beings, beautiful, lively, and beneficent in their intercourse with mortals, inhabiting a region called Fairy Land, Alf-heinner; commonly appearing on earth at intervals-- when they left traces of their visits, in beautiful green- rings, where the dewy sward had been trodden in their moonlight dances."

To the sylphs the ancients gave the labor of modeling the snowflakes and gathering clouds. This latter they accomplished with the cooperation of the undines who supplied the moisture. The winds were their particular vehicle and the ancients referred to them as the spirits of the air. They are the highest of all the elementals, their native element being the highest in vibratory rate. They live hundreds of years, often attaining to a thousand years and never seeming to grow old. The leader of the sylphs is called *Paralda,* who is said to dwell on the highest mountain of the earth. The female sylphs were called *sylphids*.

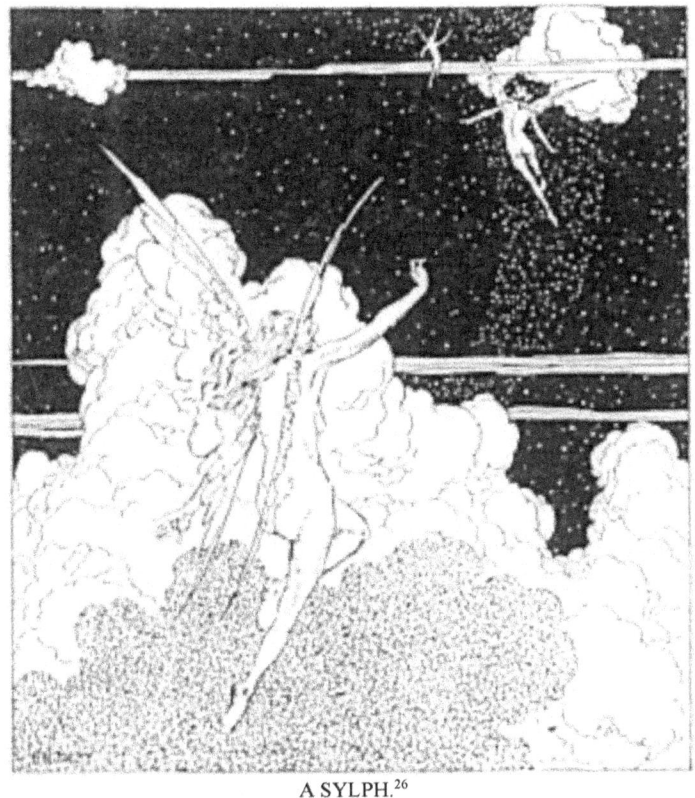

A SYLPH.[26]

It is believed that the sylphs, salamanders, and nymphs had much to do with the oracles of the ancients; that in fact they were the ones who spoke from the depths of the earth and from the air above.

---

[26] From sketch by Howard Wookey. The sylphs were changeable entities, passing to and fro with the rapidity of lightning. They work through the gases and ethers of the earth and are kindly disposed toward human beings. They are nearly always represented as winged, sometimes as tiny cherubs and at other times as delicate fairies.

The sylphs sometimes assume human form, but apparently for only short periods of time. Their size varies, but in the majority of cases they are no larger than human beings and often considerably smaller. It is said that the sylphs have accepted human beings into their communities and have permitted them to live there for a considerable period; in fact, Paracelsus wrote of such an incident, but of course it could not have occurred while the human stranger was in his physical body. By some, the Muses of the Greeks are believed to have been sylphs, for these spirits are said to gather around the mind of the dreamer, the poet, and the artist, and inspire him with their intimate knowledge of the beauties and workings of Nature. To the sylphs were given the eastern corner of creation. Their temperament is mirthful, changeable, and eccentric. The peculiar qualities common to men of genius are supposedly the result of the cooperation of sylphs, whose aid also brings with it the sylphic inconsistency. The sylphs labor with the gases of the human body and indirectly with the nervous system, where their inconstancy is again apparent. They have no fixed domicile, but wander about from place to place--elemental nomads, invisible but ever-present powers in the intelligent activity of the universe.

PART VI:
GENERAL OBSERVATIONS

Certain of the ancients, differing with Paracelsus, shared the opinion that the elemental kingdoms were capable of waging war upon one another, and they recognized in the battlings of the elements disagreements among these kingdoms of Nature spirits. When lightning struck a rock and splintered it, they believed that the salamanders were attacking the gnomes. As they could not attack one another on the plane of their own peculiar etheric essences, owing to the fact that there was no vibratory correspondence between the four ethers of which these kingdoms are composed, they had to attack through a common denominator, namely, the material substance of the physical universe over which they had a certain amount of power.

Wars were also fought within the groups themselves; one army of gnomes would attack another army, and civil war would be rife among them. Philosophers of long ago solved the problems of Nature's apparent inconsistencies by individualizing and personifying all its forces, crediting them with having temperaments not unlike the human and then expecting them to exhibit typical human inconsistencies. The four fixed signs of the zodiac were assigned to the four kingdoms of elementals. The gnomes were said to be of the nature of Taurus; the undines, of the nature of Scorpio; the salamanders exemplified the constitution of Leo; while the sylphs manipulated the emanations of Aquarius.

The Christian Church gathered all the elemental entities together under the title of *demon*. This is a misnomer with far-reaching consequences, for to the average mind the word demon means an evil thing, and the Nature spirits are essentially no more malevolent than are the minerals, plants, and animals. Many of the early Church Fathers asserted that they had met and debated with the elementals.

As already stated, the Nature spirits are without hope of immortality, although some philosophers have maintained that in isolated cases immortality was conferred upon them by adepts and initiates who understood certain subtle principles of the invisible world. As disintegration takes place in the physical world, so it takes place in the ethereal counterpart of physical substance. Under normal conditions at death, a Nature spirit is merely resolved back into the transparent primary essence from which it was originally individualized. Whatever evolutionary growth is made is recorded solely in the consciousness of that primary essence, or element, and not in the temporarily individualized entity of the elemental. Being without man's compound organism and lacking his spiritual and intellectual vehicles, the Nature spirits are subhuman in their rational intelligence, but from their functions--limited to one element--has resulted a specialized type of intelligence far ahead of man in those lines of research peculiar to the element in which they exist.

The terms *incubus* and *succubus* have been applied indiscriminately by the Church Fathers to elementals. The incubus and succubus, however, are evil and unnatural creations, whereas *elementals* is a collective term for all the inhabitants of the four elemental essences. According to Paracelsus, the incubus and succubus[27] are parasitical creatures subsisting upon the evil thoughts and emotions of the astral body. These terms are also applied to the superphysical organisms of sorcerers and black magicians. While these *larvæ* are in no sense imaginary beings, they are, nevertheless, the offspring of the imagination. By the ancient sages they were recognized as the invisible cause of vice because they hover in the ethers surrounding the morally weak and continually incite them to excesses of a degrading nature. For this reason they frequent the atmosphere of the dope den, the dive, and the brothel, where they attach themselves to those unfortunates who have given themselves up to iniquity. By permitting his senses to become deadened through indulgence in habit-forming drugs or alcoholic stimulants, the individual becomes temporarily *en rapport* with these denizens of the astral plane. The *houris* seen by the hasheesh or opium addict and the lurid monsters which torment the victim of delirium tremens are examples of submundane beings, visible only to those whose evil practices are the magnet for their attraction.

Differing widely from the elementals and also the incubus and succubus is the vampire, which is defined by Paracelsus as the astral body of a person either living or dead.[28] The vampire seeks to prolong existence upon the physical plane by robbing the living of their vital energies and misappropriating such energies to its own ends.

---

[27] which are male and female respectively
[28] usually the latter state

In his *De Ente Spirituali* Paracelsus writes thus of these malignant beings: "A healthy and pure person cannot become obsessed by them, because such Larvæ can only act upon men if the later make room for them in their minds. A healthy mind is a castle that cannot be invaded without the will of its master; but if they are allowed to enter, they excite the passions of men and women, they create cravings in them, they produce bad thoughts which act injuriously upon the brain; they sharpen the animal intellect and suffocate the moral sense. Evil spirits obsess only those human beings in whom the animal nature is predominating. Minds that are illuminated by the spirit of truth cannot be possessed; only those who are habitually guided by their own lower impulses may become subjected to their influences."

A strange concept, and one somewhat at variance with the conventional, is that evolved by the Count de Gabalis concerning the *immaculate conception,* namely, that it represents the union of a human being with an elemental. Among the offspring of such unions he lists Hercules, Achilles, Æneas, Theseus, Melchizedek, the divine Plato, Apollonius of Tyana, and Merlin the Magician.

www.ingramcontent.com/pod-product-compliance
Lightning Source LLC
LaVergne TN
LVHW041502070426
835507LV00009B/769